mahout

Illustrations by Terry Doerzaph

Cover art by *Jane A. Evans*

mahout

A keeper and driver of an elephant

HENRY M. CHRISTMAN

The Theosophical Publishing House
Wheaton, Ill. U.S.A.
Madras, India/London, England

Library of Congress Cataloging in Publication Data

Christman, Henry M.
  Mahout (a keeper and driver of an elephant)
  "A Quest book".
  "A Quest original".
  1. Spiritual life.   I. Title
BL624.C478   291.4'4   81-53008
ISBN 0-8356-0555-8 (pbk.)   AACR2

Printed in the United States of America

Mahout: a keeper and driver of an elephant.

—Webster's Unabridged Dictionary

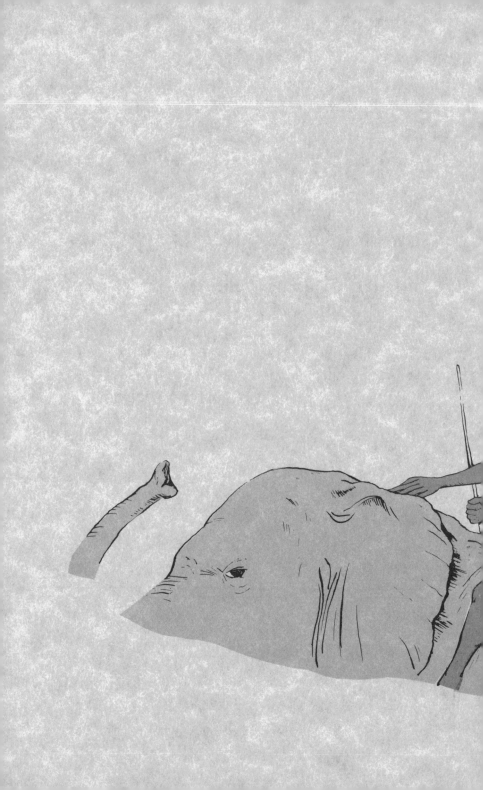

I

This little GUIDEBOOK must BE READ in a special way.

It REQUIRES putting aside acquired Western habits.

It REQUIRES the temporary BUT absolute suspension of Western thinking.

The READER must not try to REASON,

BUT

simply to feel.

Best of all, the words should be read

aloud,

slowly,

in complete privacy,

in protected solitude.

Each part is a unit. Each text must be absorbed before moving onward to the next.

II

The purpose of this guidebook is healing, and the practical application and utilization of unique Eastern experience for healing.

The word experience is used with great care and deliberation.

The initial explanation of that term is that it does not require any supernatural commitment.

What follows is intensely human, growing out of an unbroken continuity of thousands of years of human experience.

From experience, intensively tested through countless generations, comes Wisdom.

III

There is a special lesson in mountain climbing.

Each step is upward.

But each step must be secure. Each step must be tested and confirmed.

Each step must be in unison with nature. One cannot proceed — one cannot learn — one cannot succeed — unless and until the footing is secure.

The footing must be not only safe, but secure.

Reassuring security.

Comforting security.

Strengthening security.

IV

Western man and woman, and particularly Western urban man and woman, have lost contact with nature. We shall now endeavor to reestablish some of that lost contact, and that lost harmony. But it requires thinking, viewing, perceiving, and feeling in a different way.

It gives profound joy to be able to say that this ability has not been lost to us in the West; it simply requires the sincerity to reclaim it.

We shall begin with an example from holland.

During World War II, the Netherlands suffered barbaric torture and degradation; a civilized and humane and proud people were systematically and methodically stripped and robbed of everything meaningful in life. To seek truth and love justice was an offense that brought terrifying death.

Uniquely tormenting is that a living part of the Dutch people, a living limb never to be recovered, was torn away in savagery, with the deliberate, step-by-step, systematic, methodical, one-by-one murder of the Dutch Jews.

But nature, with infinite justice and infinite mercy, has given a gift of grace that lives in the heart of every Dutchman.

During the most frightful and most hopeless days of World War II the Dutch, in order to survive, had to resort to eating tulip bulbs, consuming even the rare varieties on which depended the existence and survival of species.

But the Dutch people, and their humane Dutch values, did survive.

And, with them, the tulips also survived.

Every spring in the Netherlands, the explosion of tulips of incredible variety is living proof of the triumph of good over evil, of life over death.

Every single one of those tulips has lived to fulfill its individual destiny to be alive, to flower, to reproduce, to provide beauty, inspiration, and consolation to humankind.

The reader is now asked to make the first commitment, to undergo the first experiment, and to reap the first experience of this guidebook.

the reader is asked to learn from the symbolic tulip, to share the historical destruction and the historical triumph of the tulip, and to feel and to be one with the tulip.

If you continue to read, you will learn how to do it.

V

Before man was man, man was animal.

This elementary truth is denied by many.

But it is a truth that unites the most so-
phisticated psychiatrist and the most un-
worldly mystic.

We see in everyday life the destructive
release of primitive, primal instincts, the
aggression ordinarily limited to ruthless
competition but increasingly crossing the

17

blood dangerline into violence. Civilized man seeks to control, to repress, to eliminate savage instincts.

But there is a constructive, healing part of our animal heritage that has been lost in the civilizing process. We are indeed the "human animal," and simultaneously the "animal human."

We are going to learn from our animal heritage.

VI

And now a brief pause to place in perspective that which is yet to come.

It is Wisdom from a particular part of the East, centered in the heart of Bengal.

This knowledge radiates eastward in an arc, into Malaysia, and from there into Indonesia, extending northeastward to the Sulu islands, and also southeastward to the other center of this Wisdom, the extraordinary island of Bali that is so favored, and properly so, by anthropologists, archeologists, and folklorists.

The epicenter of this Wisdom is in the mysterious hill Country of Old assam, on the border of the Sylhet region of today's Bangladesh and the Meghalaya region of India.

This is the boundary where, defined in terms of human color, the brown and yellow races meet and confront.

But it is a boundary in many ways.

It is a political boundary.

It is a boundary of races.

It is a boundary of religions.

and it is a boundary of civilization and primitivism that can hardly be imagined by Westerners. As but one example, a traveler need only continue eastward to be in tribal territory that not even the most cruel elements of the Japanese army could subdue during World War II.

It is also another type of boundary, which we shall cross when the time is ready.

VII

Let us reflect on the culture of Bengal.

The culture that is concentrated and elevated in the poetry of the Shakespeare of Bengal, Sir Rabindranath Tagore.

We can hear its ancient wisdom in the ballads of the Bauls of Bengal, the wandering bards and troubadours who continue a Minnesinger tradition long ago lost in the West.

The Bauls sing of the Old Truth.

The Old Truth relentlessly suppressed and persecuted by the orthodox.

The mystics of the East, those of the Sufi heritage, knew and protected and preserved the Old Truth.

The Old Truth still lives.

VIII

We now move into the hill Country.

Even at the height of their imperial military power, the British could not conquer the hill Country.

today, no human lives in the hill Country.

the hill Country cannot be approached by man alone. the hill Country can only be approached by man with his brother.

Man's sacred brother.

Our beloved brother.

Our Brother Elephant.

IX

But let us pause again in order to refer to our Western heritage and in order to be able to prepare ourselves better for Eastern knowledge.

Specifically, let us think back to long ago in northwestern Europe, to the Nordic and Germanic folklore generally known only through the music of Richard Wagner.

Today, those lands of Scandinavia and northern Germany are sedately Protestant. But before they were Protestant, they were Catholic. And before they were Catholic, they were otherwise.

The haunting, unforgettable films of Ingmar Bergman catch this truth, and give us a fleeting glimpse of this part of the Scandinavian and the Germanic psyche.

There are places in northwestern Europe where the Old Truth still lives, where man becomes one with nature.

It is present, too, in the Druid regions of England.

It is strong in the waves of the Baltic, where those waves crash near Viking graves.

It is strongest in the inner forests of Scandinavia, those incomparable groves which form natural grottoes enshrouding and enshrining the Old Truth.

X

But in Europe, the Old Truth, the truth of nature is now too weakened, too enfeebled, to be able to reach us, to speak to us, to teach us.

We must seek it out where the elements are stronger — in the East.

In a previous time, at an actual point of time in history, the Germanic people of northwestern Europe came into intense communication with this part of Asia.

The British colonized Bengal and Malaya, and the Dutch colonized Indonesia. Consequently, there is historical framework of relationship and relevance.

The role of time in all wisdom is paramount, and particularly so in reference to Eastern wisdom.

Our United States is little more than two centuries old. European history is, of course, much older, but it is marred by epochs of conflict and migration that have weakened the links, the ties, of man to nature, that have torn man away from his roots.

East Asian history has been quite different. The British came to Bengal and Malaya and to Sarawak and Sabah and Brunei, and the Dutch came to the major and minor islands of Indonesia. Both groups of colonialists superimposed themselves on the native populations without destroying or even comprehending the native cultures.

Yet it was the Europeans whose lifelines to home were stretched and strained to the breaking point, who were out of their element, who in the final reckoning could not retain their conquest, could not sustain their occupation.

Meanwhile, the Bengalis, the Malays, and the Indonesians had not only their culture, their civilization, their religion. They also lived with their flora and fauna and wildlife and earth that had sustained and renewed them without interruption for thousands of years.

Despised and rejected and exploited by their European overlords, the natives kept their secrets to themselves, and they hid them well. They became masters of inscrutability.

But a few Westerners have heard the
silent suffering,

    the unspoken wisdom,

       and have learned.

XI

As religion becomes formalized, institutionalized, and official, it becomes the instrument of the manipulation and control of the individual in society. Revelation is obscured and lost. Inner truth based upon basic, elemental human and animal life is lost.

The truth that we are seeking cannot be learned from the official Eastern religions as they are formally taught. Just as in the West, institutionalized religion is part of the social power structure. Indeed, in parts of the East, the formal religion not only is the official state religion, the state church, but the state exists simply as an instrument of suppression and oppression on behalf of the religion.

The answer is not there.

XII

If you have a good reference book at hand, it will tell you the major religions of the Indian subcontinent.

Hinduism, Islam, Christianity, Sikhism, Buddhism, Jainism, Zoroastrianism — and one other.

Animism.

Before any other religion, there was Animism.

XIII

Webster's Unabridged Dictionary defines animism as follows:

1. A doctrine according to which the immaterial soul is the vital principle responsible for every organic development.

2. Attribution of conscious life and a discreet indwelling spirit to every material form of reality (as to such objects

as plants and stones and to such natural phenomena as thunderstorms and earthquakes) often including belief in the continued existence of individual disembodied spirits capable of exercising a benignant or malignant influence.

XIV

Some may believe that the way to truth
that we refer to here can be approached
and achieved by the use of hashish, nar-
cotics, and other artificial means. They
should not be used, and since such means
cloud and twist the perceptions, they also
cloud and twist the truth you are seeking.

One must live with and share in and
participate in daily life, and the truths we

seek here are of greatest value and greatest use when they are applied in a totally natural way, for healing in daily life.

Nature is eternally superior, and the natural body, free of all outside agents and influences, is the best way.

XV

Remember the story of the Dutch tulip?

It sounded strange, back at the beginning of our journey, to talk about learning from a flower.

But we can learn from nature, if only we will listen.

Now we will learn from a simple bowl of rice.

Perhaps you have at one time or another savored Indonesian Rijsttafel, a delightful buffet of meats and vegetables with Eastern spices. The literal translation into English is "rice table."

There is also a literal meaning that escapes Westerners. It is the essential psychological meaning of rice to Bengalis and Malays and Indonesians.

The rice is the staple food, the basic element, and the rich meats and vegetables accompany and modify and complement the rice.

Those who modify rice only with vegetables are natural vegetarians.

Those who add meat are carnivores.

Those who are vegetarians, or seek to be, are instinctively emulating and identifying with the non-carnivore, non-violent part of the animal kingdom.

But non-violent does not mean to be without power.

Think back on the yoked oxen, plowing—

Those gentle oxen, working—

Those oxen, friends of man, working for man.

The eldest son of the non-violent ones of the jungle is Brother Elephant.

XVI

Reflect on human and animal, and their brotherhood.

feel the brotherhood.

feel the love.

This feeling has been captured by Jean Cocteau in his film masterpiece, Beauty and the Beast.

Inspired and elevated by his love for Beauty, the Beast acquires the finest of human qualities.

After hunting and slaughtering smaller, weaker animals, the Beast comes to feel anguish and remorse.

The Beast learns the quality of mercy.

Animal and human merge; they fuse and reunite and elevate.

XVII

There were two persons, two mortals, two intensely humanistic humans who were given the special knowledge, the unique gift, of fellowship and brotherhood of man with animal in fulfillment of non-violence and love.

One was from and of the West.

St. Francis.

The other was from and of the East.

Gandhi.

XVIII

"Love thy Enemy" is

    a holy teaching difficult to accept,

        a holy teaching very difficult

           to apply.

But perhaps another interpretation might serve.

There are fates that one should not and must not wish to befall even one's enemy.

If those things can be and are done to him, they can be done to you.

This is the difference, and the boundary, between civilization and barbarism.

XIX

What visitor to a good museum of archeology or anthropology has failed to be impressed by the prehistoric art in which animal and human forms are merged and fused?

These objects are said to be representations of primative gods.

Some would say that they are the surrogates of those primitive gods.

But it is also possible that they are to be, were intended to be, interpreted otherwise.

It is possible and perhaps even likely that they were and are intended to be interpreted psychologically, as implied in the title of the study, the god behind the mask.

God, however, in the animist meaning, revealing the animal and animal force in man.

XX

With those sufficiently close to nature, this animal force can be deliberately summoned and brought to the surface and released.

When the high priest puts on the mask, he is not merely worshipping an animal god or imitating the animal, but he is knowingly and intentionally and deliberately invoking, concentrating, elevating, and preparing to release the animal in himself, that he will

permit it and empower it to overcome and

dominate and possess him.

   If that mask is of a carnivore, the animal

will lust for blood.

XXI

Animal force can be brought to the surface individually or collectively.

Indonesian culture offers a remarkable example of the latter, in the ritualistic and hypnotic Monkey Dance.

By chant, music, and dance — rhythm from deep within the Indonesian legend and psyche — a group of male dancers become as one in reenacting the role of a tribe of monkeys fulfilling religious ritual.

Do not listen too long to the hissing.

XXII

In the former Northwestern frontier territories of Old India, and northwest of there, there was and still is a uniquely Eastern type of polo.

But it is not played with mallets and croquet balls.

It is played with the headless carcass of a calf.

It is a savage sport, by savage people, emanating from their savage character and history.

Reflect for a moment. When the carcass is not that of a calf, what is it?

Reflect for a moment. Where is the head?

XXIII

the powers of darkness in the animal come to the surface and are released at the moment when the snarling lips draw back, expose, release, implement the fangs.

XXIV

Now, having seen the dark side, you have learned from that darkness, and have recoiled from it, and have rejected it.

And you shall continue to move forward to healing truth.

Do not think backward. Move forward on the sacred journey, strengthened by the truth revealed to St. Francis and Gandhi.

the truth of love and harmony beyond human prejudice.

the truth of love and harmony beyond human limitation.

that love, that rediscovered love, that unites and reunites human with animal and nature.

you have now passed beyond evil.

XXV

Before man became man in his present form, he had powers that now lie dormant, lie asleep, in modern man.

Man had a sixth sense.

This truth appears in psychology and psychiatry and psychoanalysis. Theodore Reik implied this truth in his study, LISTENING WITH THE THIRD EAR.

But this sense was a separate sense, a distinct sense.

It is, yet is not, a third ear.

It is, yet is not, a third eye.

In Western terminology that sixth sense can be referred to in various ways.

The first description is instinct.

Instinct informs.

Instinct protects.

But the sixth sense is more than instinct.

It is the type of instinctive affinity known to Goethe.

Once you have rediscovered this sixth sense, this gift, you are no longer alone.

XXVI

transcendentalism:

In philosophy, any system holding that there are modes of being beyond the reach of mundane experience. The term is generally associated with Kant, who felt that space, time, and categories of judgment were transcendent — above the evidence of the senses. In American literature, a movement in New England from 1836 to 1860 is called transcendentalism. The transcendentalists — Emerson, Thoreau, Margaret Fuller, Bronson Alcott, and others — were high-minded and idealistic, laying stress on individualism, self-reliance, and social reform.

—The Columbia-Viking Desk Encyclopedia

XXVII

Think again of St. Francis, and of Gandhi.

Reflect on their gentleness, their harmoniousness.

They were gifted with childlike acceptance of people and animals.

Consider that quality that attracted animals to St. Francis.

. . . that quality that enabled Gandhi to touch and embrace the Untouchables, and make their cause his own.

. . . that quality that loves life.

. . . that quality that loves justice.

. . . that quality that does not know prejudice or bigotry.

Think on Gandhi.

Think on Gandhi as Mahatma.

Think on Gandhi as Mahout.

XXVIII

That wisdom, that harmony, that power possessed by St. Francis and by Gandhi is known by Quakers, the Society of Friends.

It is the Inner Light.

XXIX

and now you move forward, to practice what you have learned.

XXX

Ponder the function of music.

Listening to music can be a pleasing and functional implement for the exercises to follow.

If one is to follow the Indian road, then a morning Raga — only a morning Raga — may be used. This must be played solely on the Sitar.

If one is to follow the Indonesian road, then only a single Gamelan may be used, not a Gamelan orchestra.

In both instances, the intention is to catch and hold in music and spirit the first and purest rays of the sun rising in the East, for warmth and for regeneration of the moment, the day, and perhaps for eternity.

The intent is pure simplicity and simple purity.

Simply feel and accept the warmth.

XXXI

There is a second use of music.

After one has learned from the solitary Sitar, the solitary Gamelan, there is a second and different lesson from different Eastern music.

It is in the pulsing drums of a Sitar ensemble.

It is in the crashing gongs of a Gamelan orchestra.

It is in Sufi music.

It is in Dervish music.

XXXII

There is still another lesson to be learned from music.

It is in rhythm — in measured rhythm, in pulsing rhythm, in pounding rhythm.

But it is not music from man.

It is music from animal.

It can be heard in the desperate panting of the frightening, drooling, slavering wild dogs of Asia.

It can be heard in the powerful panting
of the Bengal Tiger in orgasm.

XXXIII

Consider the use of a Mandala.

Let us now, as good Western rationalists, turn back to Webster's Unabridged Dictionary:

Mandala: a graphic mystic symbol of the universe that is typically in the form of a circle enclosing a square and often bearing symmetrically arranged representations of deities and is used chiefly in Hinduism and Buddhism as an aid to meditation.

Although not known as such, the Mandala has a power known and invoked and used in the West by every religious Christian who has worn and benefited from a religious medal.

A Mandala must be comforting, and intimate, and a natural talisman in a childlike sense.

The circle enclosing the square is, in one way, simply a necklace around the neck.

But there is a dark side, and we shall reject that side. The dark side of the pentacle and the pentagram and the hexagram.

XXXIV

What is the object of pleasure?

Does pleasure strengthen love? Or does pleasure simply serve itself, drifting?

But, then, what is the meaning, and the function, of love?

XXXV

think back for a moment on the illustrations you have seen of classic hindu temple structures.

Recall the voluptuousness of the women.

these representations are no accident, nor are they products of artistic license.

Quite the contrary. Just as they seem most revealing, they carefully disguise and hide the most intimate secrets of the people of India and Indonesia.

XXXVI

But let us pause to learn from Eastern healing.

Think again of the voluptuousness, the Rubenesque voluptuousness of the Indian women in the temple sculptures.

This weight is intentional, is deliberate.

It provides the body warmth, and the power, and the force, and the pressure, for healing.

healing by Eternal Mother.

XXXVII

The wisdom of Kama Sutra is in receiving
and giving, and in giving and receiving, in
harmony, in rhythm, in the release, in the
diversification, and then the harmonious
reuniting of the senses———
the uniting of the senses—
all six of them;
the uniting of the senses—
Both sets of six of them.

XXXVIII

Consider the gift of the Mantra.

The Mantra comes from across the boundary of time, from across the boundary between life and death, from across the temporary and momentary division of the living and the dead, from the Other Part of you.

It is a simple sound. When you hear it, you will recognize it immediately.

It is a childlike sound.

It can be sensed in the songs of birds.

It can be sensed in the sudden, spontaneous smile of a child.

It can be sensed in the gurgle of a baby.

When you hear it, you will know it, and you can use it.

It will bring relaxation even under the most difficult of circumstances.

It is the trigger, the button, that opens the boundary between the living and the dead, and makes you whole with the Other Part of you.

XXXIX

Your awareness has now been brought to the point that you are ready for the exercises.

The first purpose of the exercises is to carefully and deliberately strengthen your perceptions.

The second purpose of the exercises is to help you achieve relaxation for the protection and preservation of life.

The third purpose of the exercises is for revelation of ultimate and final truth.

XL

A flower floats on the water.

You are on the banks of a lake. Floating
before you is the Sapla, the sacred water
lily, the sacred lotus of the East.

The Sapla is white.

It floats on green water.

White, the symbol of purity and hope.

Green,

the symbol of life and

regeneration.

Slowly the Sapla moves with the waves.

You watch the harmonious colors complement and blend.

You feel the harmonious and soothing motion as the flower moves — to and fro — with the water.

You recall the lesson of the tulip.

You become one with the Sapla and the water.

XLI

The first sacred gong strikes.

The sound is soft, and gentle, and pure.

The sound hangs in the air.

The sound is timeless.

The veil between the worlds, between the world of the moment and the world of eternity, rustles soundlessly.

The Gong of Eternity has sounded.

XLII

The second sacred gong strikes.

Its sound is heavier than the Gong of Eternity.

The sound pounds, and reverberates on and on and on.

It is the Gong of fate.

It is the Gong of destiny.

XLIII

You are now in Bengal.

It is not yet dawn.

The rain is falling on the tin roof. It is falling in a soothing way. The rhythm is harmonious. The rhythm is your heartbeat.

You go outside to receive the dawn.

The dawn is warming. The early rays of the sun reveal new color, the color of nature.

The color of nature is green — different greens, different greens revealing the infinity of nature.

You feel the green.

You feel the green with your eyes.

You feel the texture of the plants with your eyes.

You fondle and play with that texture with your eyes.

You have for the moment combined and merged and fused two senses, seeing and feeling.

You test and use your new gift again, in another way.

You feel the texture and the grain of wood with your eyes.

You see and feel the origin and course of river in the grain of the wood.

You have now learned to touch and feel and caress in mind and spirit; to reach across, and grasp, and hold, and hold forever, without physical contact.

You have learned how to go beyond — and grow beyond — forever.

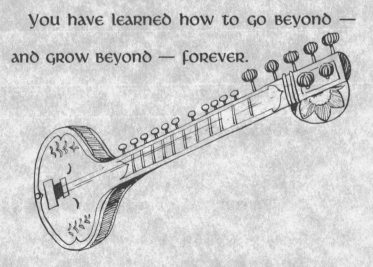

XLIV

You now understand more. You are
ready for the next exercise, and the next
truth.

The truth is coming quickly.

The comforting rain that you heard on
the rooftop, the rain that refreshed you as
you understood the plants, the rain that
you felt in unison with your heartbeat, that
rain is now raising the river.

the holy River.

You must hurry to fulfill your part in this communion with nature.

XLV

You have reached the riverbank in time.
The water is flowing, swirling, surging,
overflowing.

The water is deep green, like the plants,
in communion with the plants, in brotherhood with the plants.

The sun is just rising. You are in time.

You bathe in the water. The water is healing. And the water is now strengthened and reinforced by the Sun.

Dazzling Sun.

Golden Sun.

The Golden Sun supplements and reinforces holy Water; and Sacred Water supplements and reinforces holy Sun.

holy Water from the center of the earth.

Water made holy by prayers and, downstream, the remains of untold generations.

You are at the origin, the birth, of the holy River.

You are at the source of the holy River.

XLVI

You have been blessed with primal water.

And now you step into the strengthening, renewing rays of the Sun.

The Sun, your Brother.

You watch and admire as he gathers his strength, his power. You share in and receive and benefit from that power.

The Sun, your Brother, dries away the water and lulls you into sleep.

the Sun,

your Brother,

has warmed away

all pain, all illness, all suffering, all sin.

XLVII

You are now at final truth.

You are now in the deepest part of primitive jungle, a unique jungle that exists in reality — the majestic Sundor Bon in the Khulna region of Bangladesh.

You have been impelled there, for sacrifice, to face the Presence that exists there, that exists only there.

You are not alone.

You are astride Brother Elephant.

Brother Elephant is afraid because he knows by instinct what is to come. You can feel his massive body slightly tremble.

Brother Elephant knows the Presence in the jungle. It is his blood enemy.

The silence is total. You and Brother Elephant shiver together, waiting.

The first sign of the presence is by sound.

It is a low rumbling, as much felt as heard.

The rumbling grows into a snarl, and then a roar.

You are in the lair, the last remaining
lair, of the Royal Bengal Tiger.

the Royal Bengal tiger that is the blood enemy of Brother Elephant, and the untameable enemy of Man. the Royal Bengal tiger whose savagery, whose blood lust, cannot be tempered, cannot be modified.

You and Brother Elephant have become one, in harmony, as you look together into the glowing eyes of horrible death, and extermination, and extinction.

You are Enlightenment, and Civilization.

You are Idealism, and Justice.

You are the Inner Light.

You are the Mahout.

But as the Royal Bengal Tiger draws in his breath, and tightens his muscles, and bears his fangs, there is another sound that drifts silently in the air.

You and Brother Elephant hear it together.

It is the Mantra.

Filled with his love for you, Brother Elephant takes courage. With all his strength, he trumpets.

The Tiger pauses, and roars.

Again and again, Brother Elephant bellows, drowning out the roar of the Tiger.

The Tiger halts,

and fades back into the jungle.

xlviii

Good has triumphed over evil.

il

Love has triumphed over hate.

L

life has triumphed over death.

Quest Books

are published by
The Theosophical Society in America,
a branch of a world organization
dedicated to the promotion of brotherhood and
the encouragement of the study of religion,
philosophy, and science, to the end that man may
better understand himself and his place in
the universe. The Society stands for complete
freedom of individual search and belief.
In the Theosophical Classics Series
well-known occult works are made
available in popular editions.